CARICATURE CARVERS
Showcase

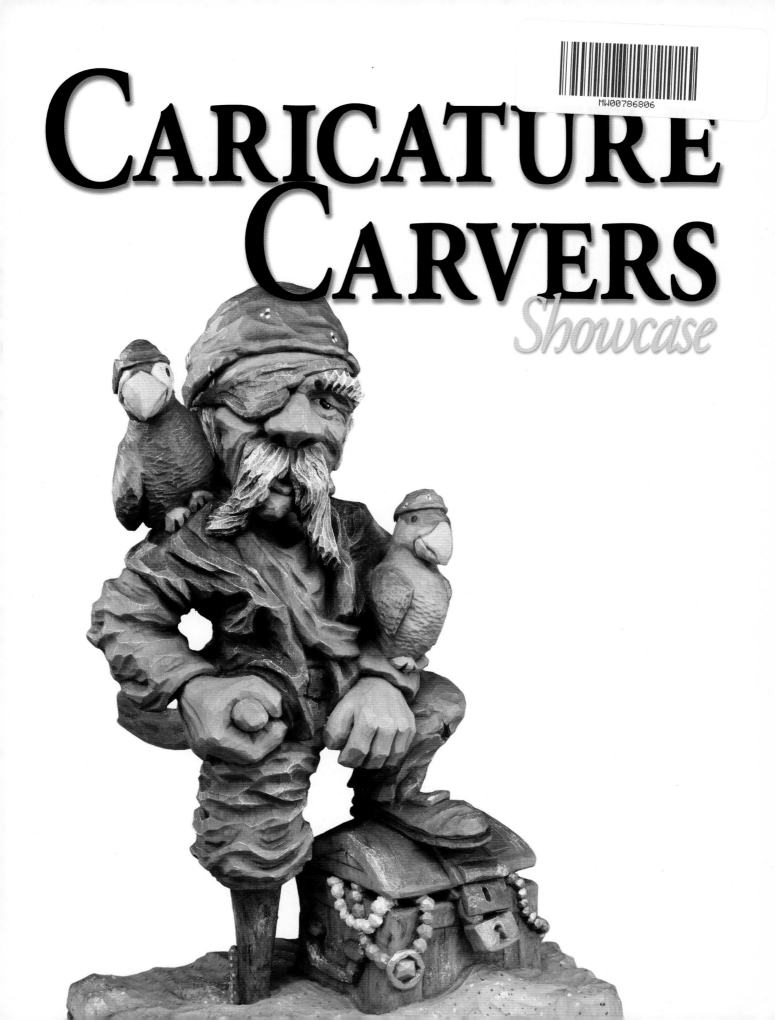

Jack A. Williams
(*) Photography

Greg Heisey
Studio Photography

Bot Roda
Illustrator

© 2007 by Fox Chapel Publishing Company, Inc.

Caricature Carvers Showcase is an original work, first published in 2007
by Fox Chapel Publishing Company, Inc. Readers may make copies of these patterns for
personal use. The patterns themselves, however, are not to be duplicated for resale or distribution under any circumstances. Any such copying is a violation of copyright law.

ISBN 978-1-56523-337-9

Publisher's Cataloging-in-Publication Data

Caricature carvers showcase. -- East Petersburg, PA : Fox Chapel
Publishing, c2007.

        p. ; cm.

        ISBN: 978-1-56523-337-9
        Summary: Features 30 caricature carvers and 50 projects,
complete with patterns and photos for guidance.

        1. Wood-carved figurines--Caricatures and cartoons. 2. Wood-
carving--Patterns. 3. Caricature. 4. Caricature Carvers of America.
I. Caricature Carvers of America.

TT199.7 .C37 2007
736/.4--dc22   0711

To learn more about other great books from Fox Chapel Publishing, or to find a retailer near
you, call toll-free 800-457-9112 or visit us at *www.FoxChapelPublishing.com*.

Printed in China
10 9 8 7 6 5 4 3 2

Note to Authors: We are always looking for talented
authors to write new books in our area of woodworking, design,
and related crafts. Please send a brief letter describing your idea to
Acquisition Editor, 1970 Broad Street, East Petersburg, PA 17520.

TABLE OF CONTENTS

This book is humbly dedicated to our good friends Claude Bolton, Dave Dunham, Tex Haase and Dave Rasmussen, whose love of caricature carving serves as an inspiration to those of us who remain.

BOLTON

Claude Bolton was truly one of the pioneers of caricature carving. His first books, *Carving Cowboys* and *Carving Heads, Hats, and Hair* were among the first on carving caricature cowboys. Claude's last book, *Carving Cowboy Faces*, is an excellent study in caricature faces. He was a nationally known instructor, and to those of us fortunate enough to know him personally, a genuinely nice guy. His support of caricature carving and his participation as a founding member in the CCA added greatly to the credibility of our fledgling organization.

DUNHAM

In addition to being generous and kind, Dave Dunham was a great caricature carver. He carved at a level to which most of us aspire. Dr. Dave had an unusually creative mind, and recognized the potential for a caricature carving in everyday incidents and ordinary interactions with people. At the time of his passing, his notebook contained ideas for dozens of carvings he had yet to transform into wood. A founding member of the CCA, Dave played an important role in the early development of the organization, serving in several key positions in our first decade.

HAASE

Tex Haase was widely known throughout the Southwest as an accomplished caricature carver and carving show judge. His carving style was a distinctive blend of caricature and realism. His carvings exhibited a unique use of subtle colors. Tex taught the art of woodcarving at the vocational school, high school, and college levels. He was a founding member of the CCA. In later years, health issues prevented him from participating in many of our activities, but he remained an enthusiastic supporter of the CCA until his passing in 2002.

RASMUSSEN

Dave Rasmussen was also a founding member of the CCA. His first love was carvings depicting the Minnesota agrarian lifestyle, carved from northern basswood. Caricature carvings of farmers, construction workers, their families, and animals were his specialty. A talented artist, Dave was equally adept at carousel restoration and sculpting larger-than-life realistic animals. Dave was an avid supporter of the CCA's mission to promote caricature carving as an art form, a subject of which he knew a great deal.

PROMOTING THE ART OF CARICATURE CARVING

In October 1990, a group of ten woodcarvers met in the back room of Paxton Lumber Company in Fort Worth, Texas, to discuss the formation of a national organization to promote the art of caricature carving. From that meeting came the Caricature Carvers of America (CCA). The founding group consisted of fifteen nationally recognized carvers, representing a broad geographical distribution, as well as diverse styles of caricature carving.

The newly formed organization made no claims of being "the best," although several of the founding members were readily recognized by the carving community as pioneers in the field of caricature carving. The same may be said of the current membership. Over the years the combined CCA membership has garnered several hundred first place ribbons, including many "Best of Show" awards in carving competitions across the nation, and two CCA members have been judged "Best of Show" at the International Woodcarver's Congress in Davenport, Iowa.

Collectively, CCA members have published over 100 books on caricature carving, and members regularly teach woodcarving seminars throughout the United States and Canada.

Since the inception of the CCA, four of our founding members are deceased, and several others have converted their membership to emeritus status (retired with honor). At this writing, six of the founding members retain active membership. New members have replaced our retirees to maintain our membership at the maximum of twenty five.

The original CCA poster created by Dave Dunham depicts the organization's 15 founding members.

Original founding members of the CCA
Front, L to R: Bolton, Rasmussen, Stetson, Dunham, Enlow
Back, L to R: Prescott, Sears, Price, Travis, Batte
Not pictured: Refsal, Hajny, Wetherbee, Haase, Kaisersatt

THE PURPOSE OF THE CCA IS TWO-FOLD:

1. To promote and elevate the appreciation of the art of caricature woodcarving within both the woodcarving community and the general public.

2. To provide an environment that will encourage growth in skill, creativity, and excellence among its members and the carving public.

To achieve these goals, the CCA has embarked on an ambitious schedule of activities including carving exhibitions, group-taught seminars, and the publication of trend-setting books on caricature carving. The CCA membership is strongly committed to education in woodcarving. Most members teach woodcarving seminars on a regular basis.

HIGHLIGHTS OF OUR FIRST 17 YEARS

The CCA's premier carving exhibit opened at the National Museum of Woodcarving in Custer, South Dakota, during the summer of 1991. That exhibit, consisting of almost fifty original carvings, returned to Custer for several years.

Carving the Full Moon Saloon was published in 1995.

Our first book, the highly acclaimed *Carving the Full Moon Saloon,* was published by Fox Chapel in 1995. The book features the work of 21 CCA members. The idea for creating a book based on the group project was conceived at the 1993 annual meeting in Wichita, Kansas. The Full Moon Saloon is currently on tour and displayed at selected Woodcraft Supply stores.

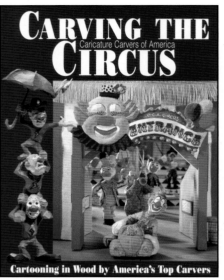

Our second book, *Carving the Caricature Carvers of America Circus,* was published by Fox Chapel in 1997 and chronicles the carving of the CCA Circus. Each active member contributed a minimum of three carvings to the circus, which totals in excess of 130 pieces.

Carving the Caricature Carvers of America Circus was published in 1997.

The CCA Signature Collection.

Our third book, *CCA Signature Collection,* features carvings from most of our current and former members. The CCA Signature Collection is currently on display at Peter Engler Designs, located in the Grand Village, Branson, Missouri. The CD book can be purchased from the "CCA Store" on our website.

In 2004 we offered a collection of CCA carvings for sale on eBay. The carvings generated funds to support our efforts in promoting the art of caricature carving. The response from the collecting community exceeded our expectations, and the auction allowed woodcarving collectors an opportunity to acquire carvings from several CCA members who do not typically sell their work.

Perhaps our most important endeavor to date was the inception of the CCA National Caricature Carving Competition. This event is open to all caricature carvers throughout the world. The first CCA competition was held in partnership with Silver Dollar City in 2002. For the next several years, the competition was held at Dollywood in Pigeon Forge, Tennessee. Starting in 2007 the competition will be held in Converse, Indiana.

As we look back over the past seventeen years, the CCA is proud to have been a part of the carving community, and to have made a contribution, however small, to the world of caricature carving. Each year we have seen the level of complexity and quality of caricature carvings skyrocket, and we have seen an explosion in the number of caricature carvings entered into competition at shows around the country. This is most apparent at the International Woodcarver's Congress and the CCA National Caricature Carving Competition. Likewise, caricature carving seminars are being offered in larger numbers, and caricature carving classes have become an important part of the curriculum of many of the larger carving seminars.

The CCA remains strongly committed to our original goals. In the coming months, we are planning several new activities that will be of interest to all caricature carvers. Watch for the details in major carving publications, on the Internet, or at our website, *www.cca-carvers.org*.

Group shot taken at the 2001 annual meeting held at Dollywood, Pigeon Forge, Tennesse. *

Gallery

Caricature is defined as exaggeration, often comical exaggeration, of reality. Whether the subject is human, animal, or another item in a scene, exaggeration is the norm. Human caricatures frequently feature oversized heads, hands, and feet. The same may be true of animal caricatures. In addition, facial expressions and other common characteristics are often fodder for the caricature carver. While caricature carvings are identified by this exaggeration, carvings must hold true to basic anatomy. A knowledge of the subject matter is necessary. Knowing which features to accentuate, and how to place the subjects in humorous poses or situations is the essence of a good caricature carving.

Caricatures come in all shapes and sizes. They depict a wide array of subject matters and represent the artist's individual sense of humor. Within this gallery you'll find a variety of carving styles and subjects to inspire you as you begin exploring this popular art form. The gallery represents original work from all past and present CCA members. We are especially pleased to showcase work from our honorarius members: Claude Bolton, Dave Dunham, Tex Haase, and Dave Rasmussen.

In the following section, all active and several emeritus members have provided projects with patterns for you to hone your skills. However, our ultimate goal is to inspire you to design your own caricatures, and to share your own brand of humor with the carving community.

GARY BATTE

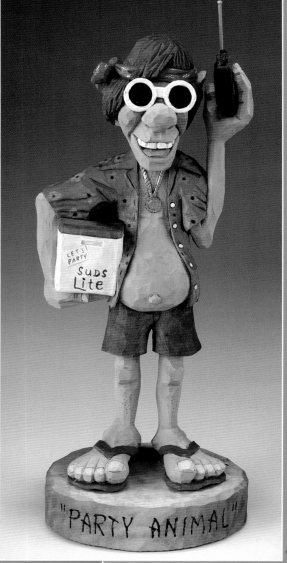

Party Animal

Say When

CLAUDE BOLTON

The Thrill of Victory—The Agony of Defeat

*
Texas Stock Exchange

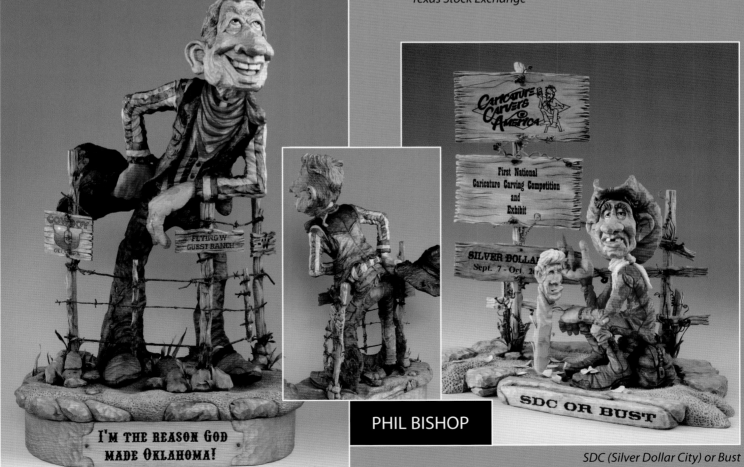

PHIL BISHOP

I'm the Reason God Made Oklahoma!

SDC (Silver Dollar City) or Bust

*

The Posse

No! Two is Load, Three is Fire!

Sports-Tater

*Butch! We shoulda used one stick with a LONG**er Fuse*

DAVE DUNHAM

*
Rock and a Hard Place

Designated Driver

HAROLD ENLOW

Mama Don't Allow No Guitar Playing Around Here!

*
Uncle Bigun

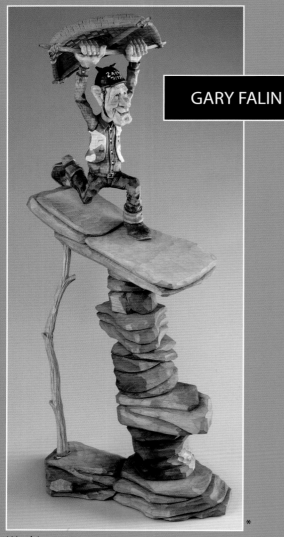

Wachis

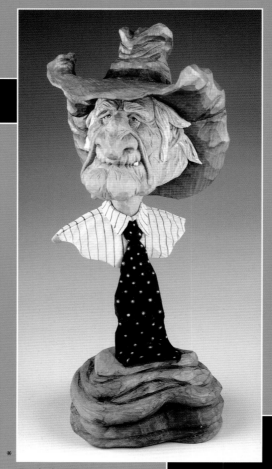

GARY FALIN

*

Duded Up

GENE FULLER

Grandpa's Tea Party

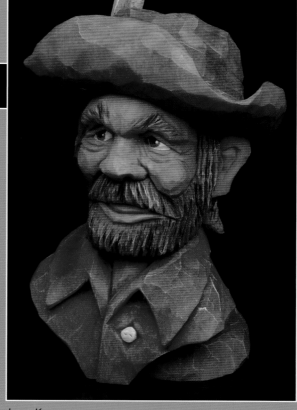

Luce Kannon

TEX HAASE

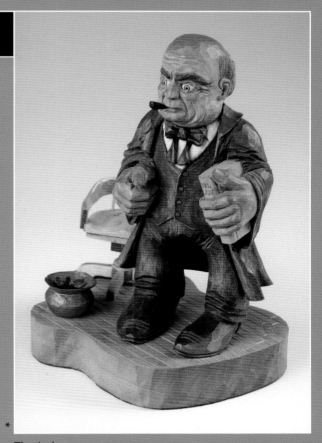

*
The Judge

*
Trouble

DESIREE HAJNY

Home on the Mange

Night Stalker

WILL HAYDEN

Skamokawa Sam *

Capt'n Ash *

BRUCE HENN

Jackpot *

Bubba Bass *

*

McJamming

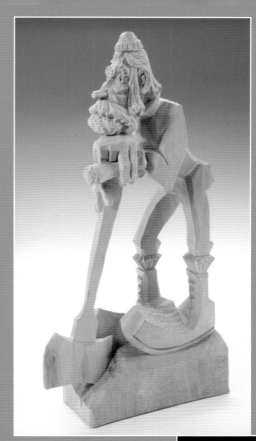

ELDON HUMPHREYS

Axeman Jacques

MARV KAISERSATT

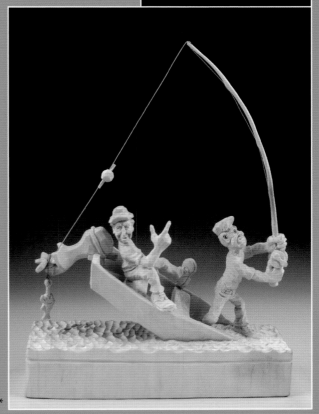

*

Where's the Ball?

*

Tale of Two Catches

Next Hold-Up I'm Getting Me a Different Horse!

RANDY LANDEN

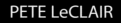

*

Putting the Cat Out

PETE LeCLAIR

Derek and Trina

Shadow Box Display

KEITH MORRILL

Wheelen Dehl

*

Doc Butcher

PETER ORTEL

Undercover Cops

*

Attitude

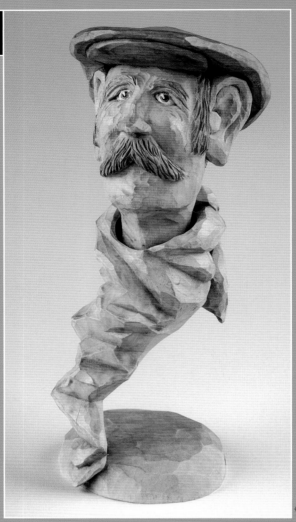

Just the Way I Like 'em

Sports Car Driver circa 1950

"I can't afford a Harley."

I Can't Afford a Harley

STEPHEN PRESCOTT

"I can tell from here, that horse don't need new shoes!"

I Can Tell From Here, That Horse Don't Need New Shoes!

*
Six Figures

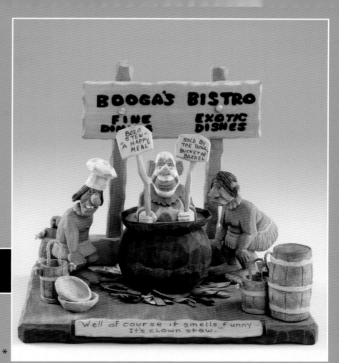

JACK PRICE

*
Well of Course it Smells Funny... It's Clown Stew

DOUG RAINE

El Burrito

Spurs

The Back Pew

Ridin' the Winter Range

Fisherman

Martin

FLOYD RHADIGAN

Harvest Queen

The Road to Mirth and Happiness

DAVID SABOL

Santa in Wonderland

Geppetto and Pinocchio

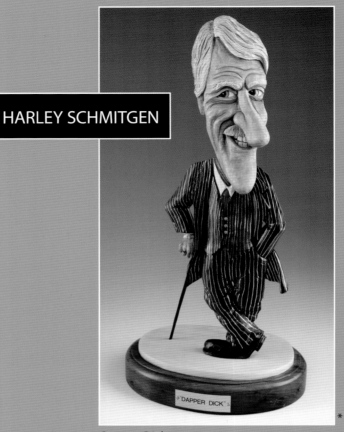

HARLEY SCHMITGEN

Dapper Dick

Lawman

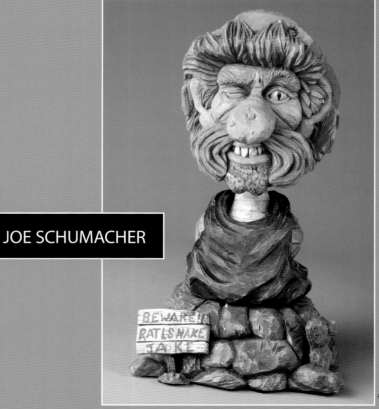

JOE SCHUMACHER

Push Me Pull Me

Beware!! Ratlsnake Jake

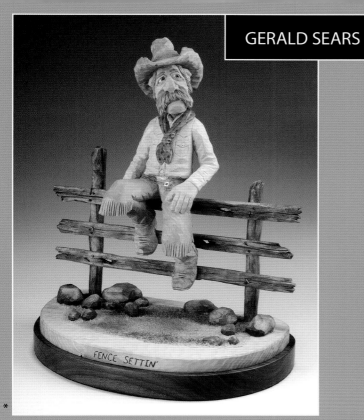

GERALD SEARS

*

Fence Settin'

*

She Said "5 Minutes," 40 Minutes Ago...

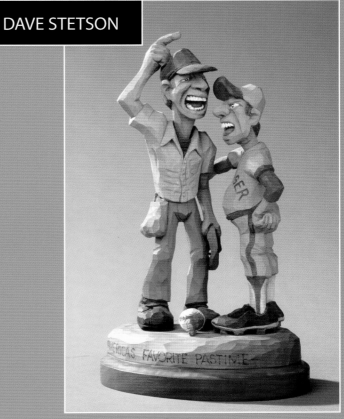

DAVE STETSON

X★!#X★@!!!...

America's Favorite Pastime

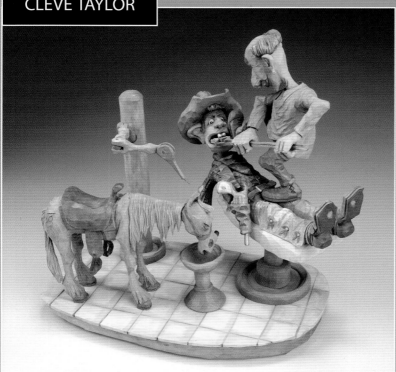

DENNIS THORNTON

Gasoline Willy

CLEVE TAYLOR

Hangin'

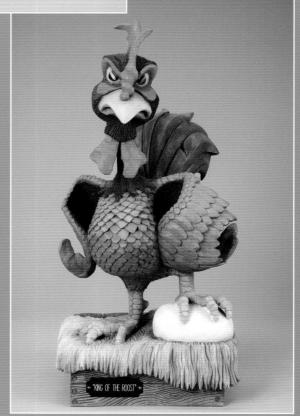

Cowboy Dentist

King of the Roost

*

I Plead the Fifth

Country Music

Edgar Ethelbert

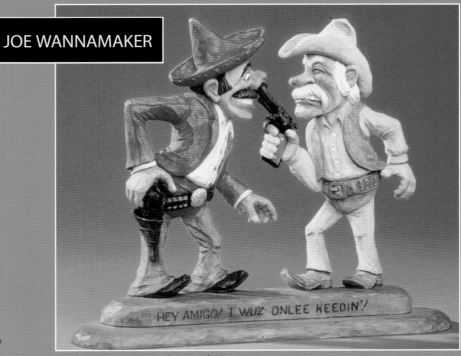

*

Hey Amigo! I Wuz Onlee Keedin'!

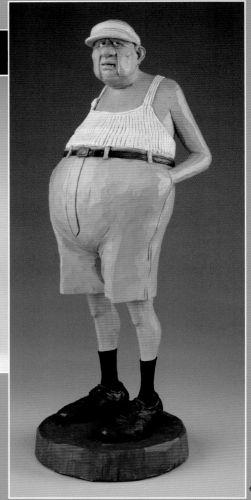

RICH WETHERBEE

*

Land Mines and Cheap Wine Blues

*

The Tourist

JACK A. WILLIAMS

*

Jester in a Phone Box

*

Ode to the Good Ole Boy

Duffer McDivot

*

* Find 'Em Boy

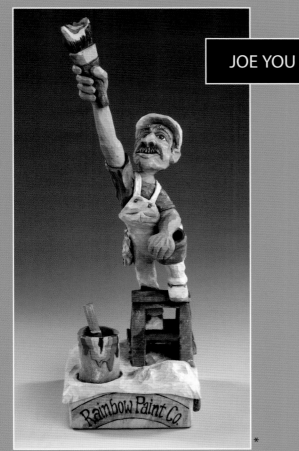

JOE YOU

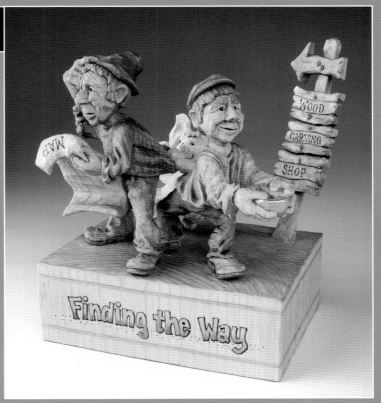

Rainbow Paint Co.

* Finding the Way

GARY BATTE

© Fox Chapel Publishing

Gary is a founding member of the Caricature Carvers of America. He has been carving, authoring books, teaching, exhibiting and selling wood carvings for over 25 years. He strives to capture a bit of humor in each of his works, and western figures are his favorites.

Gary is a 1962 graduate of Texas A&M University and retired as Area Conservationist, USDA Natural Resources Conservation Service in 1994. His work has been exhibited in many art galleries and museums including permanent display at the George Bush Presidential Library and Museum at Texas A&M University. Contact Gary at 1255 Lydia, Stephenville, TX 76401, 254-968-8793, *gabatte@earthlink.net*.

Tips from Gary Batte

This carving was inspired by the thousands of heroes who fought for the freedom we enjoy. The caricature portrays a long-retired army vet who can't quite fit into his old uniform. Make sure his belly protrudes so that his shirt and jacket are strained to the limit. When roughing out the right arm, leave some wood to support the upper part until later. Craft the "eyeglasses" from one piece of 26 gauge beading wire. Wrap the wire around a ¼" dowel to form the round portions of the frames.

OLD GEEZER
American Hero

PHIL BISHOP

Phil Bishop was born in Albion, OK and started carving in 1992. He taught himself to draw and paint, and learned to carve from books. He was elected to the Caricature Carvers of America in 1998 and became an Emeritus member in 2006.

Phil is a full-time woodcarving instructor along with his wife Vicki. They teach 25 to 30 seminars a year. Their unique style of team-teaching gives students a real bargain: two teachers for the price of one. Phil can be reached at: Bishop Collectables, 1123 West 6th Street, Elk City, OK 73644, 580-225-3109, *www.bishopwoodcarving.com*.

Tips from Phil Bishop

Wash the carving with Simple Green and water using a denture brush to scrub off any dirty spots. Paint the carving while it is still wet—do not let it dry as this will raise the grain. The paint serves as a sealer, and will prevent the grain from raising.

Use acrylic paints to paint the piece, and then rub it down with a wet piece of T-shirt. Then darken the color and shade the wrinkles, giving you three tonal values: light, medium, and dark. After the paint is dry, use a dry brushing technique to accent the clothing and highlight some of the cuts.

DAVID BOONE

DO YOU HAVE I.D.

After drawing and painting all his life, David began carving in 1984. He is a self-taught artist and designs and creates his original carvings from memories of his days growing up in the mountains of North Carolina. He says, "I like to carve scenes that show life as it should be." His carvings have won many first place awards including several Best of Show,

Show Theme, and People's Choice. David has won Best of Caricatures twice at the International Woodcarvers Congress in Davenport, IA.

David is retired and enjoys being with family and friends. He was elected to the CCA in 1997 and is a member of the National Woodcarvers Association and the Southern Highland Handicraft Guild. David is currently writing a book on his life's experience which will be published this year. Contact David at 8659 Hwy 197 South, Burnsville, NC 28714, *eboone15@verizon.net*.

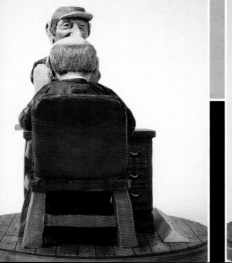

DAVID BOONE

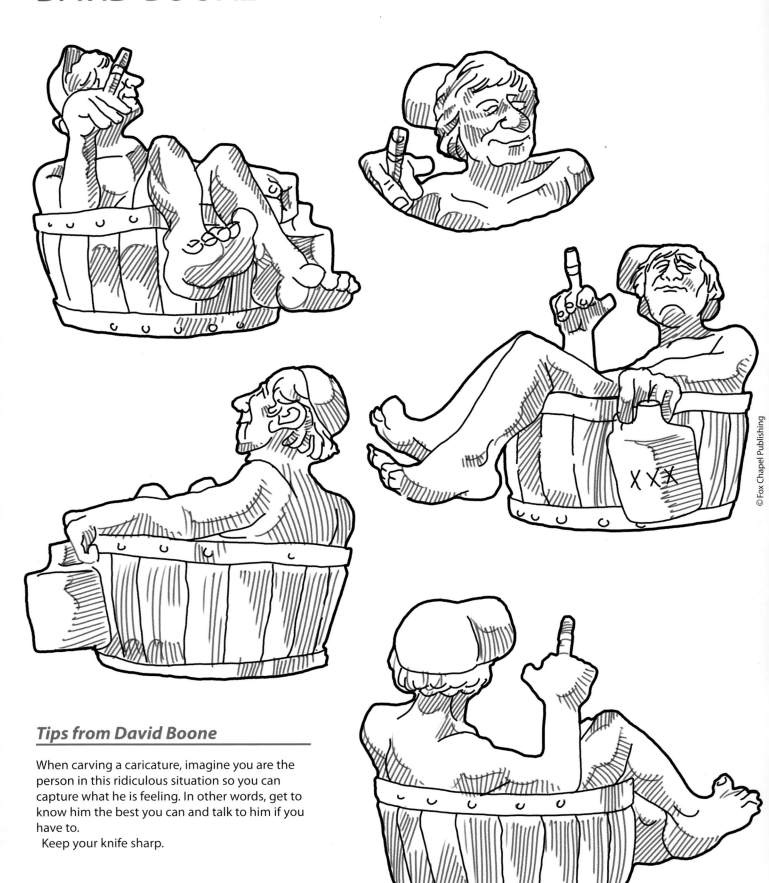

Tips from David Boone

When carving a caricature, imagine you are the person in this ridiculous situation so you can capture what he is feeling. In other words, get to know him the best you can and talk to him if you have to.

Keep your knife sharp.

TOM BROWN

Tom lives with Suzi, his wife of 32 years. He served in the Navy aboard the aircraft carrier the USS Essex. He retired early from Chrysler Corp. due to his health, so he was forced to look for something to fill his time. Along with two other scoutmasters, Tom started the Eastern Woodland Carvers Club in 1988, and he still serves as president. He was elected to the CCA in 1995.

Early classes with Harold Enlow and Ed Zinger gave Tom the desire to become a caricature carver. He was also inspired by the works of Dave Dunham and the other founders of the CCA. Contact Tom at: PO Box 221, Converse, IN 46919, *suziq@comteck.com.*

HANG NAIL

TOM BROWN

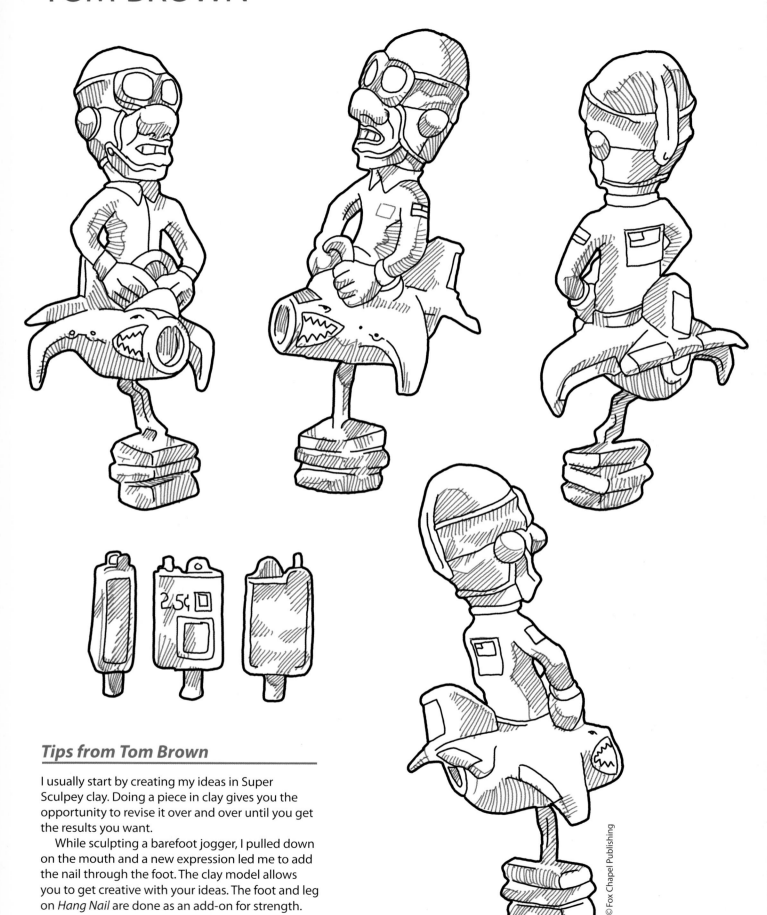

Tips from Tom Brown

I usually start by creating my ideas in Super Sculpey clay. Doing a piece in clay gives you the opportunity to revise it over and over until you get the results you want.

While sculpting a barefoot jogger, I pulled down on the mouth and a new expression led me to add the nail through the foot. The clay model allows you to get creative with your ideas. The foot and leg on *Hang Nail* are done as an add-on for strength.

HAROLD ENLOW

Harold enlisted in the Army when he was 17 years old. While in Okinawa, he found a book by H.S. "Andy" Anderson at the base library and was immediately "hooked" on caricature carving. He served during the Berlin crisis and began to carve seriously while stationed at Ft. Lewis, WA. When he returned home, he met Peter Engler, who owned a shop at Silver Dollar City, MO. Harold sold carvings through Peter's shop for a few years before opening his own in Dogpatch, AR in 1968.

He began a 30-year teaching career with his first class in 1975, and has enjoyed teaching hundreds of students. He has written several books on caricature carving. Harold and Elaine have one daughter, Katie. He is a founding member of the CCA. Contact Harold at HCR 73 Box 95-C, Dogpatch, AR 72648.

Tips from Harold Enlow

When carving hair on a female figure, use a small deep gouge. It creates a softer look than a V-tool.

Keep a box of round toothpicks with your paints. Use them to paint in corners of small eyes, highlights in eyes, dots and designs on clothing, and other hard to reach small places. Cut off the point and round the edges to make larger dots.

GARY FALIN

© Fox Chapel Publishing

After 30 years teaching troubled kids in an alternative high school, Gary retired five years ago to pursue the hobby he loves. He has been a carver for 30 years and has taught for the last 15 years. Gary is a versatile carver and has been a consistent blue ribbon winner at the International Woodcarving Congress, Dayton Artistry in Wood Show, and Dollywood. Gary won a Second Best of Show at the first CCA National Caricature Competition in 2002 and was the Best of Show winner in the 2003 CCA Competition at Dollywood.

Gary is a founding member and project leader in the Tennessee Carvers Guild. Gary says his style of carving has been greatly influenced by classes he has taken from Harold Enlow, Marv Kaisersatt, Dave Stetson, Gerald Sears, Claude Bolton, Eldon Humphreys, Pete LeClair, John Burke, Helen Gibson, and Phil and Vicki Bishop. He was elected to the CCA in 2004. Contact Gary at 693 Wright Road, Alcoa, TN 37701.

GARY FALIN

Tips from Gary Falin

Read your carving books. Don't just look at
the pictures.

When painting, think thin—except for eyes,
teeth, and metal objects. Study painting styles and
choose the one you like.

GENE FULLER

Gene taught biology at Boise State University for 33 years, retiring in 2000. He started his first carving during the Christmas break of 1998 and, with the encouragement of his wife, Jackie, he took his first carving classes the next year.

His carving style represents emphasis on realism, reflecting his study of anatomy. He is a long standing member of the Idaho Woodcarvers Guild and is currently working as one of the primary organizers of the Pacific Northwest Caricature Carvers Society (PNCCS) and its Woodcarvers Jamboree held in Twin Falls, ID. Gene was elected to the CCA in 2005.

GENE FULLER

Tips from Gene Fuller

Always use a center line to maintain balance. Make sure the leg and arm lengths are the same on each side, and that the hands and feet are the same size. Remember that you always have yourself as a model. Study yourself in the mirror or snap a photo to use as a reference.

Place a pencil horizontally on the indent at the bridge of your nose. Notice that your eyes are actually below the bridge of the nose. To ensure symmetry, draw a straight line from the inside corner of the eye to the outside corner for each eye. Compare the position of the lines while looking at the carving from different angles.

DESIREE HAJNY

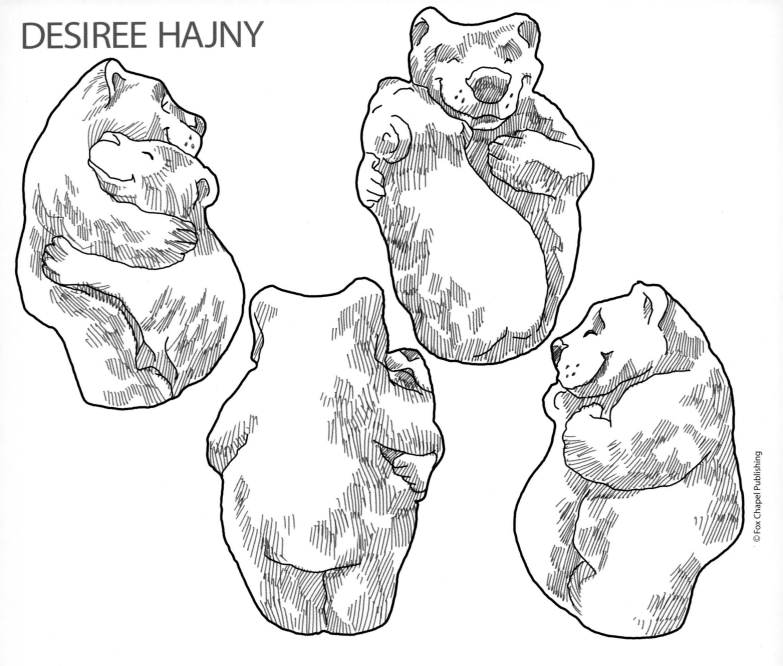

Desiree has been involved in carving full time since 1985. Currently an emeritus member of the Caricature Carvers of America, she was an original member of the organization in its inception.

Before launching her full time carving career, she was a high school art teacher. She has written and contributed to numerous books on carving. In 2003 she was named Carver of the Year by *Woodcarving Illustrated*. While still competing she garnered seventeen Best of Show and People's Choice awards and over 100 first place awards.

Desiree continues to travel through North America instructing, serving as a judge in competitions, and giving talks on her art. Contact Desiree at PO Box 191, Blue Hill, NE 68930, 402-756-3832, *hajny@gtmc.net*.

Tips from Desiree Hajny

Mama Bear Hug was carved out of a goose-sized wooden egg. The fur is done with a woodburning tool equipped with a writing tip. This provides clean, veiner type cuts on such a small project.

The texture on the nose and nostrils of the bear is made with a writing tip or ball tip. You can also achieve this effect on the hollow in the ears and the splits between the fingers. The woodburning tool makes the effect quicker than hand tooling.

WILL HAYDEN

Will was born and raised in Virginia and North Carolina. He was assigned to Fort Vancouver, WA, while serving in the Army Medical Corps. Will retired from the workforce and active woodcarving after more than 30 years of carving, judging, and teaching.

Will and his wife, Kay, a noted bird carver, spend their days in the shop, power carving at one end and whittling at the other. They still go to a few shows a year, including the Columbia Flyway Show in Vancouver, WA, that Will started in 1988. He was elected to the CCA in 1996. Will has a few patterns and step-by-step demonstrations on his web site, *www.willhayden.com*.

Tips from Will Hayden

Cut just the side view of your carving on the band saw. This gives you extra wood to remove, but allows you to change your carving as you go along. For example, you can change from a doctor to a bartender with little effort. Start carving with the largest tool you can. I use the Ortel "U" gouge

or a ¾"-wide #3 gouge, both made by Denny Tools. You'd be surprised at how far one tool can take you.

Don't hesitate to try out a new idea when carving, painting or finishing. Remember that each carving is just practice for the next one.

BRUCE HENN

Bruce has been woodcarving since 1970. Woodcarving has been his passion from the first time he picked up a knife and put it to wood. When he first began carving, he tried many styles and types of carving, but quickly developed a love of carving caricatures. He enjoys the humor, especially the public's reaction to his style of carving. He enthusiastically promotes caricature carving to anyone who will listen.

He is a member of the Woodcarvers Guild in Dayton, OH; the Brukner Society of Nature Carvers of Troy, OH; National Woodcarvers Association, Cincinnati, OH; E.W.C.C. of Converse, IN; Affiliated Woodcarvers Ltd., Davenport, IA; and was elected to the CCA in 2006.

Bruce teaches caricature carving, judges woodcarving shows, and demonstrates caricature face carving whenever asked. He is also a Boy Scout merit badge counselor.

Tips from Bruce Henn

Use a V-tool to make your initial stop cuts. Then you can adjust your lines. After the lines are established, use a knife to make deep stop cuts on those lines. The deep cuts will help stop watered down paint from bleeding over the lines.

Water down your paint. You can always add a second coat for a darker color.

ELDON HUMPHREYS

Eldon Humphreys, of Guelph, Ontario, is a retired Chief Superintendent of the Ontario Provincial Police. When he started carving in 1983, he found that caricatures fit right in with his ability to see the humorous side of things. He initially used caricature to show the funny side of police work and has since become better known for his Scottish carvings, which reflect his heritage. Carving and teaching carving have become a way of life for him.

Winters are spent in Naples, FL, where he is a member of the Golden Gate Carving Club. He is Past-President of both the Mississauga and Lake Huron Wood Carvers and a former Vice-President of the Ontario Wood Carvers. He is a member of the Affiliated Wood Carvers and the National Wood Carvers, and was invited to become a member of the Caricature Carvers of America in 1996.

ELDON HUMPHREYS

Tips from Eldon Humphreys

When the arms, hands and legs must be carved crossgrain, it makes them more liable to break. Leave them attached to an adjacent section while roughing out, and only cut them loose for final detailing.

Get the basic shape of the carving completed before you attempt to carve the details. Don't be too anxious to add the details; enjoy the complete process.

MARV KAISERSATT

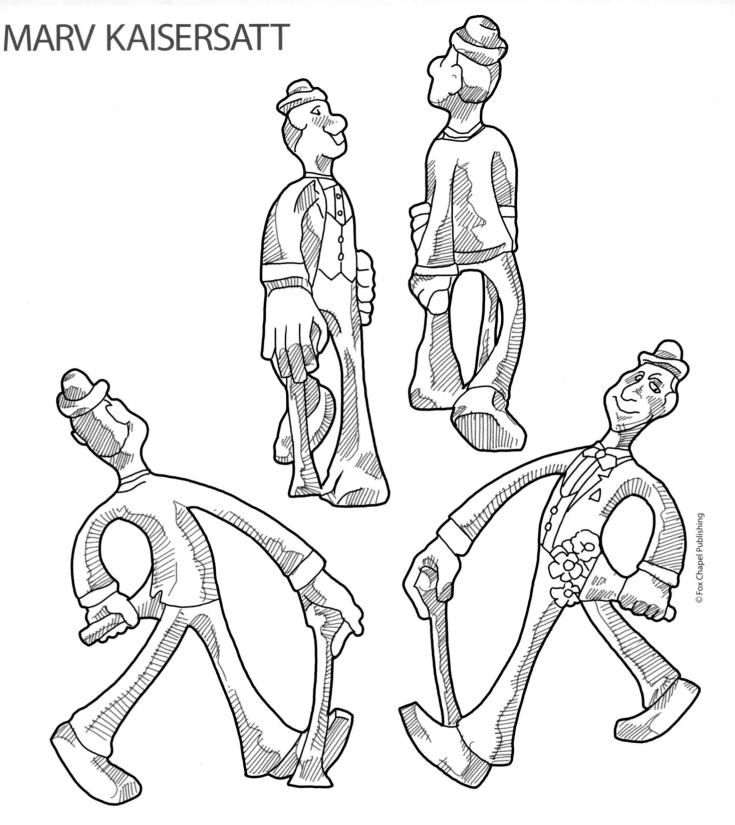

After leaving the U.S. Army, Marv taught junior high math until his retirement in 1995. He started carving in 1976 and prefers the challenge of carving scenes from a single block of wood. This allows the carving to take on a sculptural quality through the interplay of mass and space. He wrote a book,

Creating Caricature Heads in Wood and on Paper, which includes a detailed procedure for designing.

Marv was named the 2006 *Woodcarving Illustrated* Woodcarver of the Year and has won a variety of awards and honors from the International Woodcarvers Congress in Davenport, IA. He is a founding member of the CCA. Contact Marv at 227 Central Avenue, Faribault, MN 55021, 507-332-7912.

MARV KAISERSATT

Tips from Marv Kaisersatt

I use Plasteline clay to make a model for my carvings. The model is your "go by." They give you a chance to rehearse before the carving begins.

There is no right or wrong way to carve or finish a caricature. Take a chance and try something different. Your own style will emerge. Carve and finish in a way that satisfies you. Pay attention to realistic proportions, especially the head; then, carve caricatures that deviate from these proportions. Stretch beyond your carving comfort zone.

RANDY LANDEN

Randy began carving in 1990 at the Woodcarving Rendezvous in Branson, MO. His carvings are heavily influenced by his early instructors: Dave Dunham, Harold Enlow, Chris Hammack, Gerald Sears, Harold Turpin, and Ed Zinger. The ideas for his carvings come from the odd, and sometimes humorous events he has seen during his 26 years on the job at the Wichita Police Department. Randy was elected to the CCA in 1994.

He regularly instructs at the Woodcarving Rendezvous in Branson, judges at various shows, and has given carving and painting seminars across the United States. Contact Randy at P.O. Box 565, Derby, KS 67037, *rlanden@prodigy.net*.

RANDY LANDEN

BATH 5¢
BAPTIZIN

5¢
'TIZIN
FREE

Tips from Randy Landen

You can learn more in one seminar than a year of trial and error. Find the carver whose work you'd most like to emulate, and take lessons from him or her. Instructors can only teach you what they know, so learn from the best.

I don't know all of the technical details of angles and bevels, but I have learned to sharpen my tools so they work well for me. Find a sharpening system that works, and learn to sharpen. It will improve your work and make carving more fun.

PETE LeCLAIR

Pete lives in Gardner, MA. He served four years in the U.S. Navy. Upon discharge he attended Peterson School of Steam Engineering, and received an Operating Engineering license. Pete has been carving since 1973, and was stimulated to try caricature carving after watching a local carver, Al Verdini, give a demonstration. He discovered the Andy Anderson book *How to Carve Characters in Wood* and knew right then

that's what he wanted to do.

Pete started conducting seminars in the North East in 1990, since then he has conducted seminars throughout the United States, Canada, Australia and England. He was elected to the CCA in 1994. Shortly after that, he wrote his first book, *Carving Caricature Heads and Faces*, followed by *Carving Caricatures from Scratch*, and *Carving Caricature Busts*. Contact Pete at *peteleclair@comcast.net*.

Note: the A&K on Pete's hat are for his lovely granddaughters, Amanda and Kaitlyn.

PETE LeCLAIR

Tips from Pete LeClair

Observe your subject matter (people watching), and know your attention span, or how long you can spend on the carving before you start to lose interest.

Learn to sharpen the tools. Master the use of a few tools and purchase the best basswood available. Practice, practice, practice and practice more.

KEITH MORRILL

Keith is a retired Associate Professor of Biology from South Dakota State University. Keith become actively involved in carving about 25 years ago. He was particularly influenced early on by the work of Andy Anderson and Claude Bolton. Only after attending a variety of classes and seminars did carving become a "serious endeavor." Since retirement, it has been his full-time hobby.

Keith has taught numerous carving classes and has been the Carver-in-Residence at the National Museum of Woodcarving in Custer. He was elected to the CCA in 1993. Contact Keith at 12057 Fjerdingren Pl., Custer, SD 57730, 605-673-3024, *kmorrill@gwtc.net*.

KEITH MORRILL

Tips from Keith Morrill

I use water-based antiquing, available where acrylic hobby paints are sold, because I don't like the smell, mess, and drying time that you get with linseed oil. I seldom follow the directions on the tube or bottle, but thin the antiquing solution considerably just like I do the paint. You can also use very, very thin brown paint.

Waxing gives a nice look and feel to a carving. I use melted paste wax or liquid wax applied with a tooth brush. Let it dry for 5 or 10 minutes, then brush it with a clean shoe brush.

VIC OTTO

Vic began carving in 1988. He had been building fly rods and tying flies, and was looking for a new hobby. His wife, Laura, purchased an Old World Santa and a series of lessons from veteran carver, Don Brigham, as a Christmas present. The combination of camaraderie and working with his hands was all it took for him to fall in love with woodcarving.

Caricature carving seemed to be a natural path because it fit in with Vic's sense of humor. Vic enjoys mixing real-life detail and exaggeration within the same carving.

Vic has served as president of the Idaho Woodcarvers Guild and as chairman of the annual Competition and Exhibition. He was elected into the CCA in 2000. Contact Vic at 12565 W. Lewis & Clark Dr., Boise, ID 83713-0013, 208-375-8197, *vicotto@clearwire.net*.

VIC OTTO

Tips from Vic Otto

When painting the glint on the eyeballs, I prefer to use a very small brush rather than a stylus. A brush provides a small slanted "dash" rather than a dot. The glint should be placed above the equator of the eyeball with both being in the same relative position on the eye.

Remember the basics: Learn how to sharpen your tools, keep your tools sharp, and always wear your carving glove.

STEPHEN PRESCOTT

Stephen Prescott has been carving since 1981. He discovered Harold Enlow's *Carving Ozark Caricatures* book and it was love at first site. Stephen was a professional educator with nearly 30 years experience in teaching biology and coaching football. He began teaching caricature carving in 1987 and has taught classes in more than 25 states and Canada.

Stephen is a co-founder of the CCA and served as its first president. His wife, Pat, is an active partner in his woodcarving activities. Contact Stephen at Cowtown Carving Company, 5930 Plum Street, Suite 130, Watauga, TX 76148, 817-714-2160, *shpccc@aol.com*.

STEPHEN PRESCOTT

Tips from Stephen Prescott

Acrylic paint should be thinned to a consistency of a stain or wash so the wood grain shows through. To test if the paint is thin enough, paint on a newspaper. If you can still read the newsprint, it's usually okay. White is the only color I don't thin.

I use Sharpie Ultra Fine Point permanent markers for small details. Allow them to completely dry before applying the finish. I add an antiquing solution which is a combination of Boiled Linseed Oil, Odorless Turpenoid, and Burnt Umber Artist Oil to bring out the wood grain and seal and protect the finish.

BUBBA

Redneck I.D.

DOUG RAINE

Doug Raine first put sharpened steel to wood as a 10-year old. Too young for military service during WWII, Doug served as a deckhand on a Great Lakes freighter. When he graduated from Oberlin College in OH, Doug joined the Air Force and roared into the skies in an F-84 Thunderjet fighter bomber. While serving an instructor pilot tour stateside, he met and married Bobbie, his wife of 53 years.

He gave up life in the air in favor of teaching young people to aim high, first as a public school teacher and later as an administrator. When Doug retired, he took up woodcarving full time. He continues to teach and host carving seminars with some of the country's top carving instructors. He was elected to the CCA in 1993. Contact Doug at 8411 LaCanada, Tucson, AZ 85704, 520-297-2105.

DOUG RAINE

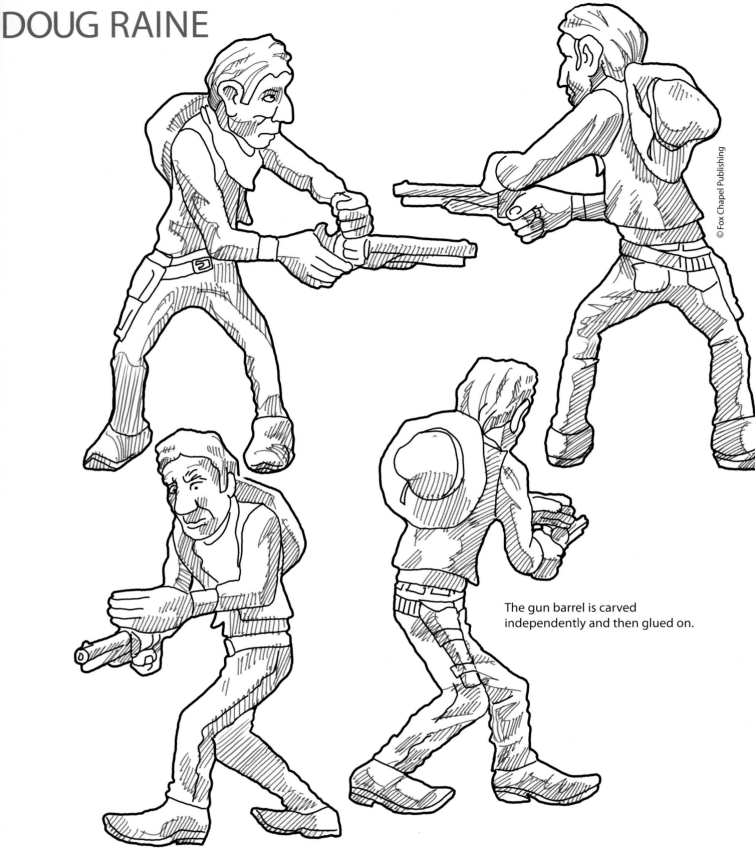

© Fox Chapel Publishing

The gun barrel is carved independently and then glued on.

Tips from Doug Raine

When I begin my piece, I find it best to carve the outside dimensions first and then work to the inside, letting any hole evolve as I go along.

"Brownie" was finished with a diluted linseed oil and, over the years, has collected dust. "Big Iron" was finished with a single coat of wax and remains dust free.

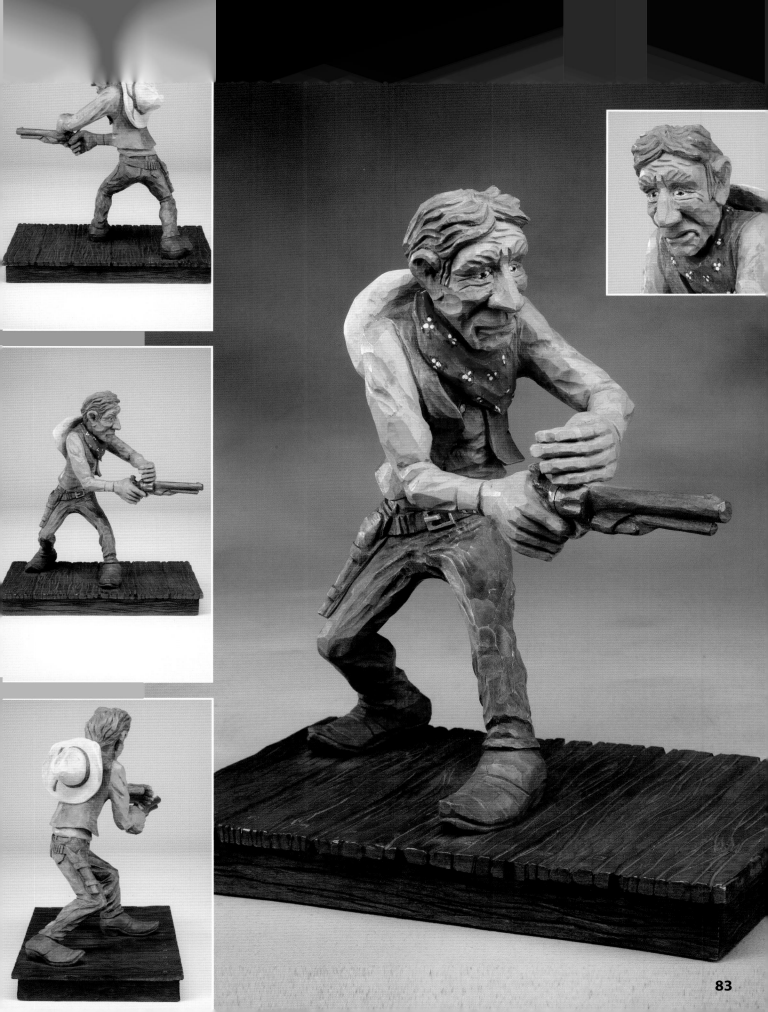

HARLEY REFSAL

Harley Refsal is considered the torchbearer of Scandinavian-style "flat plane carving," a minimalist style of figure carving that leaves tool marks exposed. An active wood carver since the late 1960s, he has taught courses in Scandinavian-style figure carving throughout North America as well as in Norway, Sweden and Iceland.

Over the past two decades he has written several books, numerous book chapters, and many magazine articles on Scandinavian carving. In 1996 Refsal was decorated by the King of Norway for his contributions to Norwegian folk art studies.

In addition to his carving, writing and seminar-teaching, Refsal is a professor of Scandinavian Folk Art at Luther College in Decorah, IA. He is a founding member of the CCA. Contact Harley at 621 North Street, Decorah, IA 52101, 563-382-9383.

Tips from Harley Refsal

Rough carve the entire figure first to define the overall shape. Then carve off the corners, so if you cut the figure off at the waist, the end view of both halves (viewed from the waist looking up, and from the waist looking down) would resemble an octagon. The same principle holds true for the head and arms—a cross section view of each would resemble an octagon. I strive for understated shape and form rather than an abundance of detail.

FLOYD RHADIGAN

Floyd entered the world of woodcarving in 1970, with the help of a family friend, Smokey Joe Briemuiller. In 1973, Floyd bought his first carving book, *How to Carve Characters in Wood* by H.S. "Andy" Anderson. Then he discovered Harold Enlow's *Carving Figure Caricatures in the Ozark Style*. Floyd started to develop his own style, a mix between Ozark and flat plane Scandinavian carving.

He began to teach his style of carving in 1976. He now instructs annually at the Wood Carvers Round Up, in Evert, MI, and the North East Carvers Round Up, in Honesdale, PA.

Woodcarving has opened many doors for Floyd. He feels the biggest honor in his career was being elected to the CCA in 2006—the group all his heroes belong to. Contact Floyd at 734-649-3259, *rhads@comcast.net, www.fantasycarving.com.*

FLOYD RHADIGAN

Tips from Floyd Rhadigan

Carve at least 30 minutes a day, every day. You will
not believe how much you will progress.

   Carve with as many good carvers as you can.
You will learn something new from them all.

DAVID SABOL

David's skills range from caricature, animal, bird, and flower carvings to human form sculptures. A traditional carver who uses knives, chisels, and oil stains, his work has a unique quality that is easily identified. He conducts 12 to 15 seminars each year with many students returning for multiple classes. David has authored several books and has been featured in numerous articles. Since becoming a full-time carver in 1983, David has received many Best of Show awards at carving shows and wildlife art exhibitions. He was elected to the CCA in 1997. Contact David at 678 Bull Run Road, Wrightsville, PA 17368, 717-252-9363, *www.davidsabol.com*.

Tips from David Sabol

Try to give your carvings a "rhythm of line." Curving and rounding of shapes and forms will give your carvings a comfortable, more natural pose. Carve away all the flat surfaces, and carve curving lines instead of straight lines to give a visual rhythm, or flow, to your pieces.

Use a three tone painting method to complement your carving and add life to the colors. For Santa's coat, use a mid range red for the coat, then a darker red or ultra marine blue for shadows, like in the creases and folds. Finish with a cadmium red light for highlights, such as the tops of the folds.

HARLEY SCHMITGEN

Harley has been in the art field since he was 19 years old. His first attempt at wood carving was carving roses in relief with a sand blast machine. He started carving basswood with knives and chisels in 1971.

He was elected to the CCA in 1991, and teaches 13 to 14 seminars a year with his wife, Midge, who is also an avid woodcarver. Over the years both his style and technique have changed. He currently is specializing in 2" deep, free-standing relief, featuring a variety of subjects, creating them to appear as if they were carved in the round. Contact Harley at Art 'N Wood Studio, 218 Oak Knoll Ct., Blue Earth, MN 56013, 507-526-2777, *harley@bevcomm.net*, *www.harleyandmidgewoodcarving.com*.

HARLEY SCHMITGEN

© Fox Chapel Publishing

Tips from Harley Schmitgen

Always start with sharp tools and buff them often during carving. You want to make good clean cuts. Never attempt to put in eyes without resharpening. This help prevents tearing and breakage.

Have good reference materials such as photos or live models. If you carve a face and know something is wrong, but can't quite figure it out, take a digital picture, and look at it on your computer. Most times this different perspective will allow you to see what is wrong.

"SONNY LET ME TELL YA"

JOE SCHUMACHER

Joe got interested in woodcarving watching carvers demonstrate at the Valley Road Woodcarving shop at Silver Dollar City in Branson, MO. He was hesitant to give it a try until years later when his wife bought him a set of carving tools, some wood, and a Harold Enlow book.

He quickly understood the benefit of taking classes and practicing. He has taken several classes with members of the CCA. He has taught classes and judged at several woodcarving shows. Joe was elected to the CCA in 2005. Contact him at 1838 Hermitage Dr., Imperial, MO 63052, 636-464-8385, *jfshoes@sbcglobal.net*.

Tips from Joe Schumacher

If you are unsure about a specific aspect of a carving, go to a practice piece of wood first and work it out there.

When carving fingernails, I use a small gouge to set a stop cut at the bottom of the nail. Then I use a very sharp knife in an arcing motion to cut from the top down to the stop cut. Using a ⅛" V-tool, I follow up the arc to the top of the nail and undercut the end of the nail to separate it from the tip of the finger.

GERALD SEARS

Gerald has been a woodcarver for over 40 years, and a woodcarving seminar instructor for over 25 years. With a life-long interest in art, he is a self-taught carver, learning many of his skills while working at Silver Dollar City, near Branson, MO. There he learned how to use and sharpen tools,

and how to "feel" the grain of the wood.

Gerald is a full time woodcarver, and teaches seminars along with his wife, Barbara. He is a founding member of the CCA. Contact him at G. & B. Sears Woodcarving, 6765 South State Highway 43, Southwest City, MO 64863, 417-762-3643, *gnbsears@netins.net*, *www.gnbsearswoodcarving.com*.

BOSS MAN

GERALD SEARS

© Fox Chapel Publishing

Tips from Gerald Sears

I carve most of my heads separately. It makes it easier to turn the heads, and gives the carving more character. If you don't like the face you carved, you can carve another one. After the carving is painted, the head is glued in place. I also carve some of the smaller items, like belt tips and spurs separately. I carve them out of tupelo, because it is stronger than basswood. After carving the tupelo to shape, you can soak it in water. Then it can be bent and twisted, almost like rubber, to the shape you want. Clamp it around a dowel and let it dry.

PONDERIN'

DAVE STETSON

Dave Stetson, cocreator and founding member of the CCA had a vision, along with carving buddy Steve Prescott, to form a group of top caricature carvers whose purpose would be to promote and elevate the public's perception of caricature carving. That was in 1989 and along with 13 other guys and gal with the same purpose, the CCA began.

Dave is a full-time woodcarver who teaches his brand of caricature as an exaggeration of realism. In order to exaggerate realism, you have to know what realism is, including anatomy, proportion, structure and form. Dave lives and works in Scottsdale, AZ with his longtime partner, and recent wife, Michele Carville (also a woodcarver).

His first book, *Caricature Carving from Head to Toe*, is available for sale. To purchase an autographed copy or schedule a seminar, contact him at 5629 E. Sylvia Street, Scottsdale, AZ 85254, 480-367-9630, *Lcnmichele@AOL.com*.

© Fox Chapel Publishing

DAVE STETSON

Tips from Dave Stetson

Know your subject matter. If it isn't in your brain, it can't be created by your hands.
    Practice, practice, practice.

SADDLE SORE

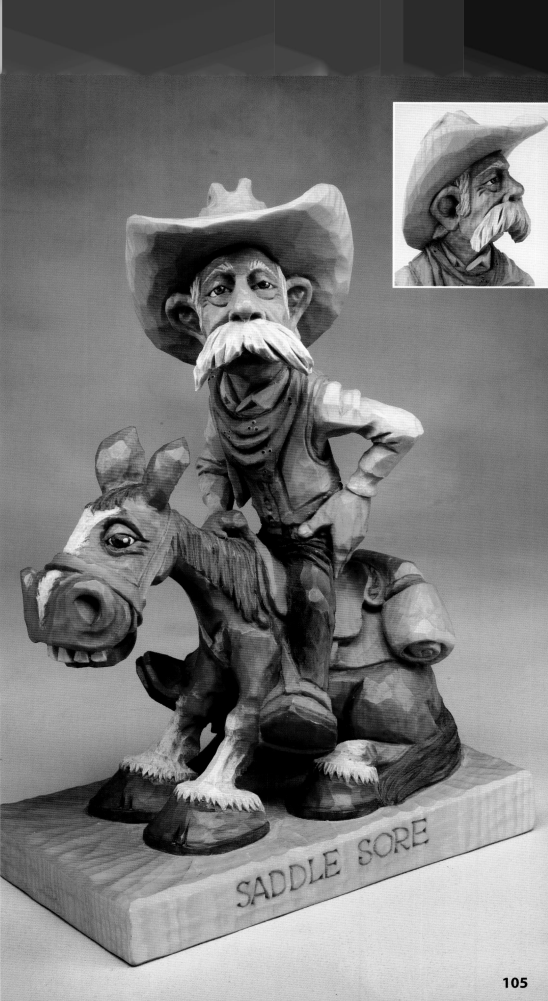

SADDLE SORE

DENNIS THORNTON

© Fox Chapel Publishing

Dennis started carving in 1995 when he enrolled in woodcarving classes. It was not long before he discovered caricatures and their unique humor. He enrolled in as many caricature carving seminars as time and money would allow.

He continually tests his skills by entering carving competitions and displaying his sculptures at exhibits and galleries. His carvings have been very well-received and have garnered Best of Show, People's Choice, and Carver's Choice honors.

Dennis was elected to the CCA in 2000. Along with his wife, Susan, he enjoys teaching carving and painting from his home studio and around the country. Contact Dennis at 439 County Road 36, Guilford, NY 13780, 607-895-6311, *splaters@hotmail.com*, *www.splintersandsplatters.com*.

DENNIS THORNTON

Tips from Dennis Thornton

Creating your own space that doesn't need to be dismantled after every carving session will increase the amount of time you carve. If there are small children, the only thing you need to put away is your tools.

Anytime I pull my tools out to carve, I take my strop out with them. It is not uncommon for me to strop my knife every 15-20 minutes of carving. This may sound excessive, but once you develop the habit, you will find a sharper tool and an easier day of carving.

BOB TRAVIS

Bob Travis retired from the University of California, Davis, where he was a professor of agronomy. He has been carving for more than 30 years. Early on, he tried several carving styles, but he soon focused on caricature carving. He especially enjoys the humor and is delighted when his carvings draw a smile from observers. Bob is a founding member of the CCA, has served as president and was the project editor on *Carving the Full Moon Saloon* and *Carving the CCA Circus*.

Bob has instructed at the Doane Experience in Crete, NE since 1990. In addition he has taught seminars at numerous locations around the country. He spends most of his free time in his carving studio in Montana. Bob can be reached at *rltravis@ucdavis.edu*.

Tips from Bob Travis

Know the realistic proportions of your subject matter. Develop an understanding of realistic proportions of the face and body. It is difficult to "exaggerate reality" if you don't understand reality.

Test the sharpness of your knife by cutting across the grain on the end of a stick of basswood. If the cut surface looks wet, your knife is sharp. It the cut surface appears cloudy or is scratched, your knife needs attention.

HAPPY HOUR

Bob
Travis
2007
CA

HAPPY HOUR

JACK A. WILLIAMS

Jack is a retired commercial photographer. He began carving in 1973 and competed with his bird carvings at the Ward World Wildfowl Competition for ten years. His first exposure to caricature carving was a Harold Enlow class in 1988. He has won several awards including Best of Show, People's Choice, the Lee Perkins Award, and the prestigious Ron Ryan Award. Jack was elected to the CCA in 2003. He spends a great deal of time photographing carvings and his images have appeared on the covers of several magazines. He is the co-author of *Carving Found Wood, Extreme Pumpkin Carving, Illustrated Guide to Carving Tree Bark,* and *Carving Cypress Knees.* Contact Jack at *carolejack@cox.net.*

JACK A. WILLIAMS

HENS
WEAR
DAILY

Tips from Jack A. Williams

To create an original carving, work your ideas out with a clay model before you start. Photograph a friend wearing similar clothing and standing in the same position to get reference material for posture and wrinkles and folds. Clothing should have realistic characteristics.

Get the carving blocked out before you start carving detail. Pencil in reference marks to provide yourself a road map. As you carve the marks away, add new ones to show any change in course. Do not do any undercutting until you complete all details. Know when to quit.

TOM WOLFE

© Fox Chapel Publishing

Tom began carving at the age of 12. A recognized and respected carver, he has helped thousands of people develop their skills and enthusiasm for woodcarving.

In addition to teaching, he has written more than 50 books which have been well received by everyone from the newest learner to the most seasoned veteran. His books provide straightforward, simple methods and step-by-step demonstrations. They are highlighted by the obvious enjoyment Tom brings to his art. He was elected to the CCA in 1992. Contact Tom at 658 Upper Hanging Rock Road, Spruce Pine, NC 28777, 828-766-2671, *tomwolfewoodcarver37@yahoo.com*.

TOM WOLFE

Tips from Tom Wolfe

Don't be afraid to try something new. Keep an open mind. If a form starts coming out of the wood, go with it. The only thing you stand to lose is the price of the piece of wood. There is always another face behind the one you are carving.

I prefer a carved base. Make it as good or better than the carving itself. A good base will enhance a carving just as a bad or dull base will detract from it. I once heard someone say that the base does nothing but keep the carving from falling over. I disagree—a poor base may cost you a ribbon!

JOE YOU

It all began when Joe stumbled upon a woodcarving show in 1991. He bought a knife, some wood, and a Ron Ranson Santa Carving book and he was hooked. He first took caricature classes in 1994. It was an incredible experience that forever influenced Joe's commitment to caricature carving.

Joe was elected to the CCA in 1998 and enjoys encouraging woodcarvers to design their own original carvings. He teaches a very simple method for making an armature to carve a human figure. Contact him for more information.

Joe is a general dentist. He and his wife, Chris, have three adult children. Contact Joe at 6373 Faustino Way, Sacramento, CA 95831, 916-392-8247, *joeyou1@comcast.net*.

JOE YOU

Tips from Joe You

When starting a carving project, don't be in a rush to start carving wood. Take time to visualize the piece. Determine what areas will need extra wood like a hat, or tie blowing in the wind, so you don't end up carving off wood that is needed.

Do not carve any detail until the carving has a close form to the finished piece. If you are carving from a class piece or a "go-by," use a pencil or ruler to gauge lengths such as width of shoulders or distance between ground and knee, etc.

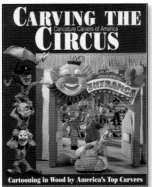
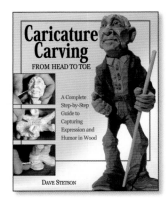

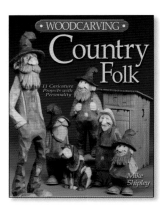

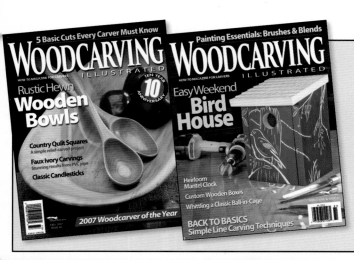